HAL•LEONARD
INSTRUMENTAL
PLAY-ALONG

AUDIO
ACCESS
INCLUDED

PLAYBACK+
eed • Pitch • Balance • Loop

TENOR SAX

MOTOWN CLASSICS

T0071689

To access audio visit:
www.halleonard.com/mylibrary

Enter Code
5701-1901-9346-2741

ISBN: 978-1-4584-0559-3

HAL•LEONARD®
CORPORATION
7777 W. BLUEMOUND RD. P.O. BOX 13819 MILWAUKEE, WI 53213

For all works contained herein:
Unauthorized copying, arranging, adapting, recording, Internet posting, public performance,
or other distribution of the printed or recorded music in this publication is an infringement of copyright.
Infringers are liable under the law.

Visit Hal Leonard Online at
www.halleonard.com

CONTENTS

ABC

TENOR SAX

Words and Music by ALPHONSO MIZELL,
FREDERICK PERREN, DEKE RICHARDS
and BERRY GORDY

© 1970 (Renewed 1998) JOBETE MUSIC CO., INC.
All Rights Controlled and Administered by EMI APRIL MUSIC INC.
All Rights Reserved   International Copyright Secured   Used by Permission

small notes optional

AIN'T NO MOUNTAIN HIGH ENOUGH

TENOR SAX

Words and Music by NICKOLAS ASHFORD
and VALERIE SIMPSON

© 1967, 1970 (Renewed 1995, 1998) JOBETE MUSIC CO., INC.
All Rights Controlled and Administered by EMI APRIL MUSIC INC.
All Rights Reserved   International Copyright Secured   Used by Permission

BABY LOVE

TENOR SAX

Words and Music by BRIAN HOLLAND,
EDWARD HOLLAND and LAMONT DOZIER

© 1964 (Renewed 1992) JOBETE MUSIC CO., INC.

All Rights Controlled and Administered by EMI BLACKWOOD MUSIC INC. on behalf of STONE AGATE MUSIC (A Division of JOBETE MUSIC CO., INC.)

All Rights Reserved   International Copyright Secured   Used by Permission

ENDLESS LOVE

TENOR SAX

Words and Music by
LIONEL RICHIE

Copyright © 1981 by PGP Music, Brockman Music and Brenda Richie Publishing
All Rights for PGP Music Administered by Intersong U.S.A., Inc.
International Copyright Secured   All Rights Reserved

HOW SWEET IT IS
(To Be Loved by You)

TENOR SAX

Words and Music by EDWARD HOLLAND,
LAMONT DOZIER and BRIAN HOLLAND

© 1964 (Renewed 1992) JOBETE MUSIC CO., INC.
All Rights Controlled and Administered by EMI BLACKWOOD MUSIC INC. on behalf of STONE AGATE MUSIC (A Division of JOBETE MUSIC CO., INC.)
All Rights Reserved   International Copyright Secured   Used by Permission

I CAN'T HELP MYSELF
(Sugar Pie, Honey Bunch)

TENOR SAX

Words and Music by BRIAN HOLLAND,
LAMONT DOZIER and EDWARD HOLLAND

© 1965, 1972 (Renewed 1993, 2000) JOBETE MUSIC CO., INC.
All Rights Controlled and Administered by EMI BLACKWOOD MUSIC INC. on behalf of STONE AGATE MUSIC (A Division of JOBETE MUSIC CO., INC.)
All Rights Reserved   International Copyright Secured   Used by Permission

I JUST CALLED TO SAY I LOVE YOU

TENOR SAX

Words and Music by
STEVIE WONDER

© 1984 JOBETE MUSIC CO., INC. and BLACK BULL MUSIC
c/o EMI APRIL MUSIC INC.
All Rights Reserved   International Copyright Secured   Used by Permission

I'LL BE THERE

TENOR SAX

Words and Music by BERRY GORDY,
HAL DAVIS, WILLIE HUTCH
and BOB WEST

© 1970, 1975 (Renewed 1998, 2003) JOBETE MUSIC CO., INC.
All Rights Controlled and Administered by EMI APRIL MUSIC INC.
All Rights Reserved   International Copyright Secured   Used by Permission

MY CHERIE AMOUR

TENOR SAX

Words and Music by STEVIE WONDER,
SYLVIA MOY and HENRY COSBY

© 1968 (Renewed 1996) JOBETE MUSIC CO., INC., BLACK BULL MUSIC and SAWANDI MUSIC
c/o EMI APRIL MUSIC INC. and EMI BLACKWOOD MUSIC INC.
All Rights Reserved   International Copyright Secured   Used by Permission

THREE TIMES A LADY

TENOR SAX

Words and Music by
LIONEL RICHIE

© 1978 JOBETE MUSIC CO., INC. and LIBREN MUSIC
All Rights Controlled and Administered by EMI APRIL MUSIC INC.
All Rights Reserved   International Copyright Secured   Used by Permission

MY GIRL

TENOR SAX

Words and Music by WILLIAM "SMOKEY" ROBINSON
and RONALD WHITE

© 1964, 1972, 1973, 1977 (Renewed 1992, 2000, 2001, 2005) JOBETE MUSIC CO., INC.
All Rights Controlled and Administered by EMI APRIL MUSIC INC.
All Rights Reserved International Copyright Secured Used by Permission

STOP! IN THE NAME OF LOVE

TENOR SAX

Words and Music by LAMONT DOZIER,
BRIAN HOLLAND and EDWARD HOLLAND

© 1965 (Renewed 1993) JOBETE MUSIC CO., INC.
All Rights Controlled and Administered by EMI BLACKWOOD MUSIC INC. on behalf of STONE AGATE MUSIC (A Division of JOBETE MUSIC CO., INC.)
All Rights Reserved   International Copyright Secured   Used by Permission

THE TRACKS OF MY TEARS

TENOR SAX

Words and Music by WILLIAM "SMOKEY" ROBINSON,
WARREN MOORE and MARVIN TARPLIN

Moderately, with feeling

© 1965, 1967 (Renewed 1993, 1995) JOBETE MUSIC CO., INC.
All Rights Controlled and Administered by EMI APRIL MUSIC INC.
All Rights Reserved   International Copyright Secured   Used by Permission

WHAT'S GOING ON

TENOR SAX

Words and Music by RENALDO BENSON,
ALFRED CLEVELAND and MARVIN GAYE

© 1970 (Renewed 1998) JOBETE MUSIC CO., INC., MGIII MUSIC, NMG MUSIC and FCG MUSIC
All Rights Controlled and Administered by EMI APRIL MUSIC INC. on behalf of JOBETE MUSIC CO., INC., MGIII MUSIC, NMG MUSIC and FCG MUSIC
and EMI BLACKWOOD MUSIC INC. on behalf of STONE AGATE MUSIC (A Division of JOBETE MUSIC CO., INC.)
All Rights Reserved   International Copyright Secured   Used by Permission

YOU'VE REALLY GOT A HOLD ON ME

TENOR SAX

Words and Music by
WILLIAM "SMOKEY" ROBINSON

© 1962, 1963 (Renewed 1990, 1991) JOBETE MUSIC CO., INC.
All Rights Controlled and Administered by EMI APRIL MUSIC INC.
All Rights Reserved   International Copyright Secured   Used by Permission